Signs

Brenda Stein Dzaldov and Cheryl Urback

I went to the mall with my family. We saw a lot of signs. Mom said, "Some of the signs tell us the rules."

We saw this sign.

Mom stopped the car.

That's the rule.

We saw this sign.

We didn't bring our dog.

That's the rule.

PLEASE USE HAND RAIL

We saw this sign.

We held on to the handrail. That's the rule.

NO FOOD OR DRINKS, PLEASE

We saw this sign.

We ate our snacks outside the store.

That's the rule.

We saw this sign.

We slowed down.

That's the rule.

We all made signs at home.